To the Rescue

Written by Mary-Anne Creasy

Flying Start
to Literacy®

CONTENTS

INTRODUCTION

Rescue workers save people's lives. They save people who are trapped in dangerous or difficult places.

Rescue workers are trained to work in dangerous places. They are also trained to keep themselves safe.

Rescue workers are always ready to go when someone is in danger. It is part of their job to always be ready.

Chapter 1

FIRE RESCUE

Firefighters are always ready to fight fires.

When there is a fire, the firefighters get into the fire truck. They use the siren so they can get to the fire quickly.

At the fire, firefighters work fast. They may have to rescue people who are trapped in a house fire or a bushfire.

They wear special clothes to protect themselves from the heat of the flames. They wear masks to help them breathe when there is lots of thick smoke.

Meet a firefighter

My name is Mick. I remember one time when we got a call at the station – there was a house fire. We drove as fast as we could with the siren on. I put on my air tank and mask. I was ready!

At the house, someone was trapped inside. I smashed down the door with my axe. A woman was on the ground and couldn't breathe. I carried her out of the house and she was okay.

My job is dangerous, but I love it because I know that with every fire I could save a life.

Chapter 2

SEA RESCUE

It is dangerous to rescue people from the sea. Often the weather is bad and the waves are big.

People who have to be saved at sea are often very tired and weak.

Helicopters are used to rescue people at sea. Rescue swimmers are trained to jump out of a helicopter and swim to people to help them.

Meet a rescue swimmer

I became a rescue swimmer so that I could save lives. I never think about the danger because of my training. I just think about saving the person who is in danger at sea.

One of my most dangerous rescues was during a storm. A man was hurt in a boat and had called for help.

I jumped into the freezing water and swam to the boat. I helped the man into the rescue basket. The helicopter took him to hospital.

It makes me proud to say that I saved his life.

Chapter 3

FLOOD RESCUE

When there is lots of rain, floods can happen fast. Roads and houses can get washed away. People can be trapped in their houses or their cars while water rises quickly around them.

Rescue workers have to work quickly to save people who are trapped. They often have to work in heavy rain and strong winds.

Brave people who are trained and know about the dangers of floods do this work.

Meet a flood rescue worker

Hi, I'm Jim. There was one time when we got a call that a man had crashed his car on a flooded road. The car was jammed against a fallen tree. The man was trapped inside his car and the water around him was rising fast.

It took a long time to get the man out of his car, because we had to work under the water and the water was icy.

But I would do it again, because when a person is in danger you only think about saving them.

Chapter 4

MOUNTAIN RESCUE

When people are lost or hurt on a mountain, rescue workers are ready to help them. If the weather is good, rescue workers use a helicopter for the rescue. But when there is a storm, they cannot use a helicopter because it is hard to see.

When this happens, the rescue workers
have to go by foot. This can take
many days in cold, stormy weather.

Meet a mountain rescue worker

My name is Mel. I remember that my first mountain rescue was very exciting. We had to rescue a mountain climber who had fallen into a large gap in the snow and was stuck.

I had to climb down a wall of ice. It was hard to see where to put my foot, but I was careful and stayed safe. We used ropes to get the climber out and then a helicopter took us off the mountain.

I am always ready to save another life.

CONCLUSION

Rescue workers do very dangerous work. They follow rules that keep them safe when they rescue people.

We are lucky to have these brave people to help us when we need saving.

INDEX